VALUE OF COUPLE UNITY IN FAMILY UPBRINGING.

Raising a progressive family.

By

Dr. TIMOTHY KESSINGTON

approval from the publisher or creator.

TABLE OF CONTENTS

TABLE OF CONTENT

Emotional enhancement/improved academic performance.

Conclusion.

ABOUT THE AUTHOR

Dr. TIMOTHY KESSINGTON is a licensed psychologist in the state of texas. he is a certified counselor on marriage and relationship/mental health. He is passionate to the core to see people in relationships happy and couples achieve the best out of every relationship

INTRODUCTION

The family is society's most fundamental and necessary institution, and raising children within a family is a significant responsibility for parents. Couples' unity is critical in this situation. The relationship between parents has a significant impact on children's development. A strong bond between parents fosters a positive family atmosphere, providing children with the emotional security they require for a healthy upbringing. We

will look at the importance of
couple unity in family
upbringing in this book.

CHAPTER 1

Unity

The state of being united, connected, and having a shared sense of purpose or goal is referred to as unity. In the context of family, unity refers to the strong bond and connection that exists between the couple and serves as the family's foundation.

Chapter 2:

Raising a Family.

The process of raising and nurturing children in a family environment is referred to as family upbringing. It entails providing emotional, physical, and social support to children to help them grow and develop into responsible, productive members of society.

CHAPTER 3

A positive Family Atmosphere.

When couples have a strong bond and unity, they create a positive family atmosphere. This environment gives children the emotional security they require for a healthy upbringing. A positive family environment can help children develop self-esteem, confidence, and a sense of belonging.

CHAPTER 4

Emotional Security.

Emotional security is the sense of safety and comfort that children feel when they are in a supportive and caring environment. Couples with strong bonds can provide their children with this emotional security, which is critical for their healthy development.

CHAPTER 5

Communication.

Communication is the process by which people exchange information and ideas. Communication between couples is essential in the context of family upbringing to create a positive family atmosphere and provide emotional security to children.

CHAPTER 6

Trust.

Trust is at the heart of any healthy relationship, including those between couples. Couples who trust each other can foster a positive family environment and provide their children with emotional security.

CHAPTER 7

Conflict Resolution.

The process of resolving disagreements and conflicts between individuals is known as conflict resolution. Couples who are skilled at conflict resolution can foster a positive family environment and provide emotional security for their children.

CHAPTER 8

Modeling.

The process of demonstrating behavior that others can imitate is referred to as modeling. Couples with strong bonds can set a good example for their children, guiding them to become responsible, respectful, and compassionate adults.

CHAPTER 9

Empathy.

The ability to understand and share the feelings of others is referred to as empathy. Couples who show empathy for one another can foster a positive family environment and provide emotional security for their children.

CHAPTER 10

Patience.

Patience is the ability to remain calm and composed in stressful situations. Couples who model patience in their behavior can create a positive family environment and provide emotional security to their children.

CHAPTER 11

Teamwork.

The ability to work together toward a common goal is referred to as teamwork. Couples with strong bonds can work as a team to foster a positive family environment and provide emotional security to their children.

CHAPTER 12

Support.

The provision of emotional, physical, and social assistance to others is referred to as support. Couples who have a strong bond can support each other and their children, creating a positive family environment and providing emotional security to their children.

Chapter 13

Emotional enhancement/improved academic performance.

Children who grow up in a home where their parents have a close relationship have better emotional well-being. They feel safe, loved, and cared for, which aids in the development of a positive outlook on life.

Children who grow up in a positive family environment

tend to outperform their peers
academically. They have a
sense of belonging and
support, which allows them to
focus on their studies and
achieve their academic
objectives.

Conclusion.

Finally, the importance of couple unity in family upbringing cannot be overstated. Strongly bonding couples can foster a positive family environment and provide emotional security to their children. This can help children grow into responsible, respectful, and compassionate citizens who can make a positive contribution to society. As a result, to ensure the healthy upbringing of their children, couples must work on

developing and maintaining
strong bonds.

www.ingramcontent.com/pod-product-compliance
Lightning Source LLC
Chambersburg PA
CBHW050754250726
48662CB00005B/2217